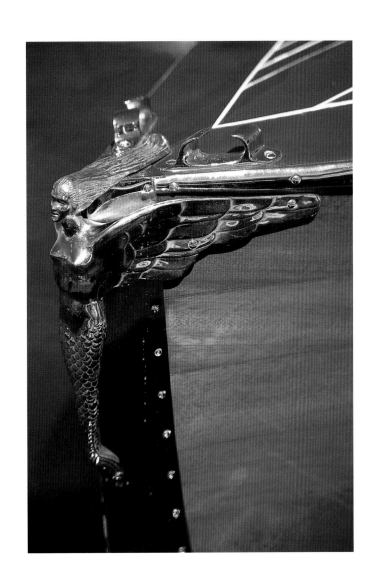

The American Wooden Runabout

Anthony S. Mollica, Jr.

POUFF
GRINDSTONE ISLE.

MBI

First published in 2002 by MBI Publishing Company, Galtier Plaza, Suite 200, 380 Jackson Street, St. Paul, MN 55101-3885 USA

MBI Publishing Company books are also available at discounts in bulk quantity for industrial or sales-promotional use. For details write to Special Sales Manager at MBI Publishing Company Wholesalers & Distributors, Galtier Plaza, Suite 200, 380 Jackson Street, St. Paul, MN 55101-3885 USA.

Library of Congress Cataloging-in-Publication Data Available
ISBN 0-7603-1143-9

Front Cover: Chris-Craft's awesome, modernistic barrel-back styling, as exhibited by this 17-foot Riviera from 1941, first appeared in the 1939 model year. *Courtesy Jack Savage*

Frontispiece: Beginning in 1930, the bow of every Dodge runabout was adorned with a graceful silver sea nymph, a throwback to their automotive heritage. *Photo by* Classic Boating *Magazine*

On the title page: Perhaps the design most frequently associated with the name Gar Wood is the triple-cockpit runabout, which was offered in standard lengths of 33, 28, 25, and 22 feet. These sleek, powerful craft—like *Pouff*, a 22-foot 1936 Gar Wood—were play toys of wealthy sportsmen from the 1920s to the start of World War II.

On the back cover: Expressly designed for the conditions on Long Island Sound, the 30-foot Sea-Lyon runabout, with its long fore deck and five-sectioned windshield, was an impressive craft that provided a remarkably smooth ride. *Photo by* Classic Boating *Magazine*. American boatmakers in the early-twentieth century often gave as much attention to their interiors and cockpits as they did their hulls, decks, and powerplants. This is the forward cockpit of a 19-1/2 foot 1941 Gar Wood.

Edited by Dennis Pernu
Designed by Liz Tufte

Printed in China

Contents

Acknowledgments

With the exception of Chris-Craft and, perhaps, one or two others, the craft of boat building didn't seem compatible with a reverence for permanent record keeping. The information void resulting from lost, discarded, and destroyed records from many disbanded boat builders will never be fully recovered. So much has been lost forever.

However, the desire to appreciate more fully the creative talent of these skilled builders of mahogany runabouts motivates the sharing of information among scores of amateur collectors. It is this extraordinary cooperation that provides researchers and authors with missing bits of information that allow us to record accurately the achievements and struggles of America's classic boat builders. Dedicated researchers depend on many private sources willing to share their collections in order to help us accurately reconstruct information as we journey back in time. Each contributor provides another valuable ingredient as we attempt to record a detailed picture of the builders that created the boats we continue to enjoy today.

Much of the content and many illustrations in this book are the result of individuals sharing their carefully preserved collections. I offer my sincere appreciation to those who contributed to this book: Bruce Bone, Jim Brown, Jeffrey Beard, Bill Feikert, Tom Frauenheim, Rebecca Hopfinger, Lindsey Hopkins, Tom Koroknay, Charles Lefebre, Paul Miklos, Harold Orchard, Jack Savage, Bill Siegenthaler, Martin Smith, Jack Teetor, David Thomas, Phoebe Tritton, Jim Wangard, Norm Wangard, Todd Warner, and Wilson Wright.

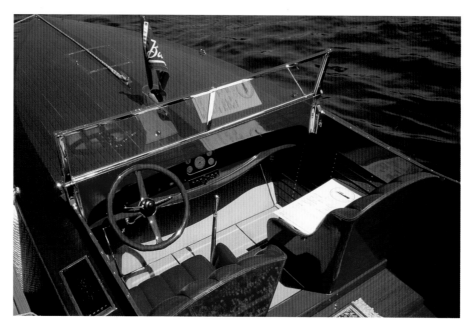

The impressive forward cockpit of a classic 33-foot Baby Gar gentleman's runabout.

Foreword

Classic mahogany runabouts are a most appropriate introduction to the world of powerboating. Often, people think only of Chris-Craft when they think of wooden boats. But, in the text that follows, the author reveals that several builders of the ever-popular runabout not only existed, but in many ways also flourished. Tony Mollica skillfully allows the reader an opportunity to sample the several varieties of runabouts and feel the seductive power of each.

When I entered the world of wooden boats through the Antique Boat Museum just six years ago, I had no idea how seductive its culture could be. Having never been connected to the boating world, I found the vastness of the material extraordinary. The types of boats, the rich personalities of their owners, and the many approaches to building were sometimes overwhelming. Tony encouraged the study of these magnificent boats, both as chairman of the Collection Committee and by his example. It was a blessing to be introduced to him early in my career. He charmingly fostered a learning experience that expanded my understanding of the many areas of watercraft.

Although the types of boats vary, there is a commonality that ties the vastly different segments of the boating world together. The link can't be touched but it's felt every time someone shares a memory, shows you their boat, or recounts an especially frustrating on-the-water experience. The bond that is formed between boat and person is so strong that it's led to emotional displays in which eyes brimmed with tears and has caused children to daydream about wild adventures on the water.

This book enables the reader to develop an appreciation for the wooden runabout and its intriguing qualities. Taking a look at the seven historical leaders in runabouts is a wonderful place from which to begin an educational journey. From the lines of boats to the stories of their makers, *American Wooden Runabouts* is a tidy package of information. For some, it will be the beginning of a never-ending love that will inevitably lead to the making of great memories.

—Rebecca Hopfinger, Curator
The Antique Boat Museum
Clayton, New York

Nostalgia, a small 16-foot Gar Wood Speedster from 1935, is evidence of the American boat industry's post–Great Depression re-evaluation of their product lines.

Introduction

Our curious love affair with old wooden runabouts didn't blossom fully until wooden boat production gradually dwindled to a trickle in the late 1960s. Some enthusiasts are convinced that our passion for wooden runabouts is greater today than during their peak production years, when beautiful tropical hardwoods were used in their construction. Today, many older mahogany runabouts are affectionately referred to as "classics." Their proud owners assume a strange responsibility to learn and recite endless details of their boat's construction, its distinguishing characteristics, and the adroit techniques of its builder. Contemporary owners of wooden runabouts appear to care more about their boats' fine points than the original purchasers did when the boats were new.

A few contemporary boat builders still specialize in constructing mahogany replicas of old runabouts.

Before 1920, many early runabouts were styled like *Pal*, a John Hacker–designed, 21-foot, long-deck model with its engine located forward of its large single cockpit. *Photo by Classic Boating Magazine*

They operate small, highly specialized shops in which one or two boats are constructed at a time. The appearance of these new runabouts may be identical to the original versions of the most popular production models. In nearly all cases, modern materials are combined with contemporary improvements in their construction, along with prudent safety features. Modern engines provide reliable power and offer far greater speeds than vintage engines. The new powerplants are lighter and more powerful, and permit many traditional hull designs to achieve the higher speeds that their designers knew were inherently possible. Owners of these new classic runabouts relish the opportunity to recapture a vision of success, fixed in time, from years passed.

Contemporary runabout builders also provide an attractive alternative to the enthusiast's time-consuming search for a reasonably healthy vintage original of a particular design. The search for a favorite boat may take years. Even when the quest is

The 19 1/2-foot 1941 Gar Wood runabout with its attractive folding V-windshield represents the continuation of Wood's pre–Great Depression edict for modern styling, as well as his depression-era focus on smaller runabouts.

Gar Wood's *Miss America II* of 1921, powered by four Liberty engines, was too extreme for the Gold Cup rules committee. The new rules that followed resulted in a "gentlemen's" runabout style beginning in 1922.

ultimately successful and that rare boat is located, the required restoration may be an unreasonable project to undertake.

Some marine historians believe the term *runabout* originated in the Thousand Islands region of the St. Lawrence River around the turn of the twentieth century. Among these islands, a variety of early motorboats provided swift transportation for wealthy residents traveling between the mainland and their island cottages. These long and narrow launches, with inboard engines located forward of their cockpits, were sleek and fast. They employed soft-riding displacement hulls powered by dedicated two-, three-, and four-cylinder marine engines. The boats "ran about" swiftly from one island to the next, making the term *runabout* seem like a perfect fit for this activity.

For nearly half a century, wooden runabouts were America's elegant jewels of motorboating. With their stylish appearance, thrilling performance, and superb craftsmanship, they were the perfect tribute to a wonderful era of extraordinary

Colonel Jesse Vincent, vice president of Packard, wins the 1922 Gold Cup in his Chris Smith–built runabout—the first boat to display the name "Chriscraft"—helping to generate enthusiasm for the runabout style.

marine development. Today, American wooden runabouts continue to captivate collectors and restorers, who scour marinas, garages, and boathouses for neglected craft they can restore to their days of glory. While examining the leading figures who contributed most to the evolution and marketing of runabouts during their prime, readers of this book will come to recognize and understand the distinguishing characteristics among the runabouts most frequently featured at today's antique and classic boat shows.

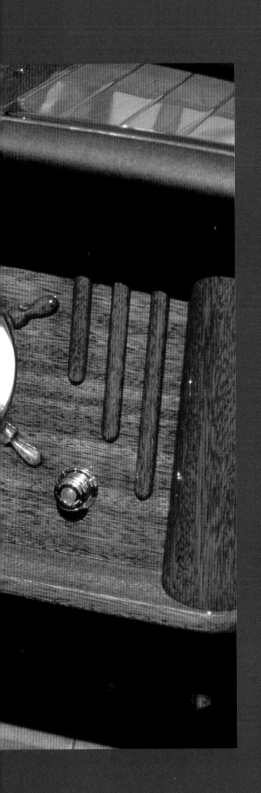

1

The Development of the American Wooden Runabout

The first motor-driven boat was built in America in 1889 and used an imported German gasoline engine. Before this, launches were powered first by steam and then by naphtha, a crude precursor to gasoline. A cumbersome boiler, belching smoke, and dangerous cinders characterized steam power. Naphtha power, on the other hand, was an improvement over steam and provided much cleaner operation. In 1891, the Pennsylvania Iron Works in Philadelphia began to produce Globe gasoline marine engines. These big, heavy engines offered modest power, but claimed excellent reliability. Gradually, with the development of the two-cycle engine over the next 12 years, gasoline-powered launches grew in popularity. One of the distinguished features of the 1901 Pan American Exposition held in Buffalo, New York, was the presence of 25 gasoline-powered launches. Truscott Boat and Engine Company of St. Joseph, Michigan, built the boats just for this event

A 22-foot Gar Wood runabout features a handsome dashboard with Art Deco styling.

With the increasing demand for automobiles, the development of the gasoline engine advanced rapidly. Boat builders soon realized that the onset of more powerful gasoline engines required them to re-evaluate their hull designs for greater efficiency. The traditional fantail stern gave way to the improved canoe stern design. In a few years the canoe-style stern was replaced by a design known as the "torpedo stern," which in turn was succeeded by the V-shaped transom. Eventually, however, the flat transom became the most universally adopted style. With time, designers found many creative ways to curve, rake, and "barrel" the flat transom into one of the distinctive features of the classic runabout.

The most recognized runabout of the 1920s was the Baby Gar 33, with its V-drive Liberty aircraft engine producing speeds up to 55 miles per hour. This powerful image became an icon among photographers and illustrators for decades. *Courtesy Roy Dryer*

The shape that symbolized the golden era of beautiful mahogany speedboats shot into popularity when the rules for the Gold Cup Trophy Regatta were changed in 1922. The year before, Gar Wood won his fifth consecutive Gold Cup Trophy race and the Rules Committee met quietly for the sole purpose of changing the eligibility requirements. Without limitations on engine size or hull configurations, Gar Wood's continued domination of the Gold Cup races seemed inevitable. Wood was already using multiple aircraft engines in his boats and was prepared to design and build a new craft every year if that was necessary to tighten his hold on the trophy. With his remarkable creativity and motivation, not to mention his wealth, he appeared unbeatable.

After a series of closed sessions, the Rules Committee shocked the boat-racing world by altering the eligibility rules governing engine size and hull configuration. It soon became obvious that the new rules were aimed directly at restricting Gar Wood's superior race boats. As a result of these changes, Wood's outstanding race boats, *Miss America I* and *Miss America II*, along with *Miss Detroit V*, were ineligible for the 1922 Gold Cup races. The committee stated their position quite simply:

> . . . [I]t is important for the good of the sport to encourage racers to use multi-purpose type boats that would be suitable for family recreation when not involved in a racing event. . . . [T]he new rules would result in boats that would cost less to build, be much safer to operate and be suitable for a variety of recreational activities when not involved in racing.

The first standardized model from the new Chris Smith & Sons Boat Company was their 26-foot runabout, introduced in 1922 for $3,500 and guaranteeing a speed of 30 miles per hour.

The plan to thwart Gar Wood's domination of the Gold Cup worked: Wood never won another Gold Cup race after the rule changes. However, one immediate result of the new rules was the desire by many sportsmen to own a fast runabout that could compete in the regatta. The types of boats that the committee encouraged came to be referred to as "gentlemen's runabouts," a name that quickly stuck. Boat builders sensed an opportunity and began to offer fast "gentlemen's runabouts" for the emerging recreational market.

The prototype for the early runabouts was a design that placed the engine behind two forward cockpits, with a third "rumble seat" cockpit located aft of the engine. The term "triple cockpit" was commonly used to describe runabouts of this style built in the 22- to 33-foot range. Runabout styling was refined in the decades that followed, as the

Cost-saving production techniques allowed Chris Smith & Sons Boat Company to achieve their objective of affordable boats for families of average income.

boats became popular status symbols for the wealthy and the watercraft of choice for thousands of sportsmen anxious to experience the thrill of speeding on lakes and rivers, to the delight of their passengers. The sight of a large runabout traveling at high speed, seemingly approaching flight on wings of water, captured the fascination of many sportsmen. Everyone who could afford one wanted a big, fast runabout of their own. Boating and boat building boomed.

By the mid-1920s many of the leading runabout builders realized that their limited production facilities restricted their potential sales volume. Gar Wood, Dodge Watercar, Sea-Lyon, Chris-Craft, and others were operating from small and inefficient facilities. Dodge was the first to announce plans to build a totally modern factory in Newport News, Virginia. Gar Wood, meanwhile, began negotiations for a prime location near Marysville, Michigan, on which to build a modern factory. As boat

The 1946 15-foot Sea Maid was Century's last split-cockpit model. *Photo by Classic Boating Magazine*

sales continued to increase, nearly every boat builder felt pressure to erect new facilities and expand production; several succumbed to that pressure. It was a great time to be in the boat business, and everyone looked forward to the 1930 New York Boat Show with unparalleled enthusiasm.

On October 29, 1929, as construction of a number of new boat factories was nearing completion, the world's stock markets began a disastrous plunge. Initially, few understood the far-reaching impact the crash would have on the world's economy. Orders for new boats came to an abrupt halt. Customers, then dealers, began to cancel their orders. Boat manufacturers were stretched to their financial limits with obligations for expanded facilities that now appeared both unnecessary and burdensome. Even well-established boat builders were soon hanging on by a thread.

The clean lines of Sea-Lyon runabouts made them some of the most appealing designs of their time, brief as that period turned out to be. *Courtesy Jack Savage*

Nearly a year earlier, Chris-Craft accepted a quarter-million-dollar deposit to sell a portion of its corporate stock to a top New York investment firm. The offer, along with a $250,000 deposit to validate it, took place months before the stock market crash. After the crash, the investors canceled the contract. Chris-Craft's carefully prepared contract held up in court and they were granted the right to keep the full proceeds of the deposit. As it turned out, the deposit was enough to help the company survive the leanest years of the Great Depression.

Likewise, the Dodge family's automobile fortune provided the financial means to support their newly constructed Dodge Watercar factory in Newport News as their boat production dropped to precariously low levels. Howard Lyon's new Sea-Lyon fleet made its grand entrance into the market just before the 1929 crash. Just when sales appeared promising, the depressed economy hit Lyon so hard that survival was impossible.

Gar Wood was in a much different position. His boat-building operation was really a small, separate division of Gar Wood Industries, and the demand for his other commercial products, which included earthmovers, tank trucks, and furnaces, remained strong despite the Great Depression. Gar Wood's boat division continued to operate with a token workforce producing a handful of new runabouts in a facility designed to build nearly 1,000 boats a year.

During this bitterly depressed period, boat builders were forced to design and offer smaller, far less luxurious models at sharply lower prices. The previously hot runabouts were all at once considered too extravagant. The only hope for survival was modestly priced smaller boats. During this time,

Mahogany is a modern, high-performance 40-foot runabout created in the classic Gar Wood style by the Turcotte Brothers, well known and respected today for their superb re-creations of traditional Gar Wood–inspired designs.

small, multipurpose craft known as utility boats began to gain popularity. The early utilities were unattractive, stripped-down models with small engines and modest speeds. They lacked all the excitement and styling of the glamorous runabouts, but were affordable and useful for sportsmen who needed boats for transportation.

2

Chris-Craft
A Vision of Popular Boating

Chris Smith was a resourceful family man who loved hunting, fishing, and boating. He was a humorous storyteller, enjoyed smoking cheap cigars, and preferred living in the small town of Algonac, Michigan, to anywhere else. He provided space in his boat shop for the Algonac Post Office to operate, and for many years served his community by holding positions on the school board and the town council.

Smith built quality duck boats, rowboats, punts, and skiffs for local sportsmen, but often spoke of building larger powerboats so affordable that the average American family could participate in boating. Each time his dream appeared attainable, however, another financial setback delayed him. When an opportunity finally arrived in 1922, Smith felt it might be too late. His sons, however, adopted his vision of affordable boats and, together, the family agreed that it was worth pursuing. The ensuing three generations of Smiths worked with unusual resourcefulness and exceptional skill to become the world's largest motorboat builder.

One of the all-time favorite Chris-Crafts is the 19-foot Custom runabout, introduced in 1939 with a fully barreled transom and top speed of 40 miles per hour. Sixty years later, it is still one of the most popular classic runabouts ever built. *Photo by Classic Boating Magazine*

The company that would become Chris-Craft was started in 1874 by Smith and his brother, Henry, both of whom were skilled hunters and popular local guides among visiting sportsmen. Recognizing a need for small, rugged boats to accommodate hunters through the marshlands around Lake St. Claire, Michigan, the brothers began building duck boats in their shop. Before long, Smith Bros. Boat Builders were installing gasoline engines in their small craft.

After a few years, Henry decided to sell his share of the business and open a grocery store. Baldy Ryan, whose primary interest was boat racing, became Chris' new partner. Their partnership lasted just two years, during which time nearly all of Ryan's money vanished through his uncontrolled penchant for gambling. With Ryan gone, Smith and his sons built a race boat named *Baby Speed Demon II* for a new customer, Stuart Blackton. Blackton won the 1914 Gold Cup race behind the

More than 1,400 Cadets were built during its three-year production run. Its success was just what the Smiths needed to reassure them that they were on the right track and could continue to expand their line with new models. This cockpit is from the model's last production year, 1930.

Prior to the war, nothing said "Lady's Man" quite like a 19-foot Chris-Craft barrel-back runabout—as evidenced by this period photo. Thanks to its thrilling performance—a 131-horsepower engine produces speeds up to 40 miles per hour—it is one of the most sought-after wooden runabouts among modern collectors.

wheel of *Baby Speed Demon II*, setting a record speed of more than 50 miles per hour. It proved a huge victory and brought instant recognition to Smith's boat shop, which was operating under a new name: The C. C. Smith Boat & Engine Company. Even with this important victory, Smith's boat business did not develop into the secure, profitable operation that he had anticipated. When Blackton's money ran out, just as Ryan's did the year before, he too left Smith with sizable unpaid accounts for work completed.

In 1915, a group of Detroit businessmen calling themselves the Miss Detroit Power Boat Association contracted Smith to build a new Gold Cup boat. The boat, named *Miss Detroit*, won the 1915 race. Although the association took great pride in the victory, just as previous racing customers had done, they left Smith with an unpaid debt. This time the debt was so critical that continuation of the family business was thrown into doubt.

About this time a newcomer entered the Detroit scene. Garfield Wood bought *Miss Detroit* at

The full-barrel transom was a vivid example of creative design and skilled craftsmanship. It is a styling achievement that still captivates the attention of runabout enthusiasts. *Courtesy Jack Savage*

an auction that was hastily organized to pay off the balance owed to Smith. After assuming ownership of *Miss Detroit*, Gar Wood agreed to finance C. C. Smith Boat & Engine Co. In return, Smith and his sons would build all of Wood's new race boats. The Smiths had become wary of race-boat enthusiasts, but Wood's flourishing dump truck–manufacturing business provided a sense of security for the new partnership.

For the next six years, from 1916 to 1922, Smith and Wood were the most productive combination in the history of the sport, winning five consecutive Gold Cups, two coveted British International (Harmsworth) Trophies, and several other races and established world speed records. Their successful partnership resulted in the Smiths' financial solvency, and in 1922 the family bought a large parcel of land for their boat-building operation. Again, the Smiths would try to fulfill their dream of building affordable, standardized runabouts, this time as the Chris Smith & Sons Boat Company.

Their first standardized model was a 26-foot runabout with a beam of 6 feet, 6 inches and was powered by a 90-horsepower Curtiss V-8 airplane engine that the Smiths converted to marine use. Curtiss engines were inexpensive and readily available from the U.S. government as World War I surplus. They also provided the 26-footer with a dependable 30-mile-per-hour speed. In 1922, the 26-foot runabout's first year of production, the Smiths sold 24 units for $3,500 each. The following year, 33 were sold. In 1924 the deck configuration was changed to a true triple-cockpit style and 48 were sold. In 1925, the Smiths added a windshield and sales increased to 111 units, followed by 134 in 1926, by which time the price had dropped to $2,900.

At the 1927 National Motor Boat Show, the Smiths added a second runabout to their line-up by introducing their 22-foot Cadet. The standard model, offered for $2,250, was powered by a 70-horsepower Kermath engine that produced speeds of 30 miles per hour. More than 1,400 Cadets were built during its three-year production run. Its success was just what the Smiths needed to reassure

Chris-Craft's 19-foot and 23-foot Custom runabouts for 1939 and 1940 included twin "Bugatti-style" folding windshield panels that provided a refreshing breeze with a simple twist of two wing screws.

them that they were on the right track and could continue to expand their line with new models.

The following year, Chris Smith & Sons Boat Co. introduced two totally new 24- and 28-foot runabouts. In addition, their original 26-foot model could be ordered with a custom sedan top. The big news for 1928, however, was their first cruiser model, a 30-foot commuter using an enlarged runabout hull design. The major styling change for 1929 and 1930 was the introduction of an upswept deck on the 20-, 22-, 24-, 26-, 28-, and 30-foot triple-cockpit runabouts. The new deck had been designed prior to the market crash and production moved ahead, with the Smiths, like most of the nation, no doubt believing the effects of Black Monday would be short lived. The upswept deck was attractive and provided an even more distinguished appearance to their handsome runabouts.

Everything seemed to be moving along perfectly for the Smiths, who in 1930 officially

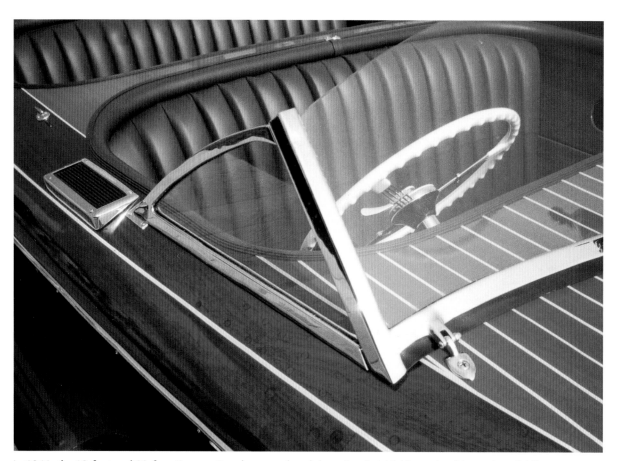

In 1941, the 19-foot and 23-foot Custom Runabouts replaced the twin windshield panels with a unique folding side-wing V-windshield. The clever design was attractive and functional, and established a totally new look for the popular runabout.

changed the name of their enterprise to Chris-Craft Corporation, having already begun using the name "Chris-Craft" in the mid-1920s to identify their boats. Chris-Craft Corporation's optimism, however, soon turned to caution: as the economy continued to falter, some stock boats were listed as "available on special order only." On the bottom of the price sheet was a note stating that these special models required "full deposit" with the order. The depression's full, destructive impact on the national economy had not yet been fully experienced.

In 1931, Chris-Craft Corp. unveiled a 17-foot runabout with a 41-horsepower engine for $1,295.

The 19-foot Racing Runabout was one of two Chris-Craft models (the second model was the Special Runabout) that received painted cedar rather than varnished mahogany planking during the early postwar years, when the exotic wood was in short supply. *Photo by Classic Boating Magazine*

When Chris-Craft resumed production after World War II, the 20-foot Custom Runabout was the company's only truly new model. With bleached mahogany creating new deck patterns flowing right into the transom, the Custom provided a tantalizing glimpse of what might lie ahead for Chris-Craft enthusiasts. The 20-foot version offered from 1946 to 1949 (this example is from 1948) is acknowledged as Chris-Craft's only advanced, totally new postwar design.

It was followed in 1932 by a 15 1/2-foot runabout for $795. The 18- and 20-foot runabouts, meanwhile, were offered in standard and deluxe versions to provide the option of reduced pricing. In 1933 it was decided to call the standard models "specials" and even offer the 15 1/2-foot runabout as a special at the reduced price of $595.

The small 15 1/2-foot runabout was upgraded in 1934. Its price increased slightly to $845 when

Chris-Craft added their first utility model to their line-up for just $495. The utility was a bare-bones craft with a tiller rather than a steering wheel.

In 1935 and 1936, runabouts were offered in six lengths—16, 18, 19, 22, 25, and 27 feet—as the marine industry began its slow return to pre-Great Depression sales levels. It would be a long, painful recovery period with many casualties, but the boat builders that survived came through with a much better understanding of what it took to keep their overhead under control. They also learned to provide the boats needed to attract new customers. No company did this more effectively than Chris-Craft.

The next five years saw significant advances in runabout design and performance, as builders began moving forward with confidence. New models incorporated attractive contours that featured woodworking artistry at its best. In 1937 the 27-foot Custom Runabout was reintroduced as the Special Race Boat with a 350-horsepower engine and speeds up to 54 miles per hour. In 1939 the awesome barrel-back styling appeared on Chris-Craft's 19- and 23-foot runabouts, along with Bugatti-style folding windshields. The creativity and flair for streamlining exhibited by Chris-Craft designers was well suited to the freedom and speed associated with the runabout's mystique. Although Chris Smith died in September of that year, his passing did not negatively affect Chris-Craft. Though he had spent nearly every day at the Algonac factory, his sons, Jay, Bernard, Owen, and Hamilton, had been in full control of production and marketing for more than a decade. They continued the modernistic trend exhibited by the barrel-back runabouts in 1941 with the barreled-bow Custom Runabout series, featuring a new folding V-windshield with hinged side wings.

The Smiths also seemed to have a good handle on world events. They were involved in government contract bidding throughout the 1930s and added additional factory facilities in anticipation of the need to build large quantities of military craft. When America went to war, Chris-Craft was prepared to completely convert its factories to wartime production. Their experience building boats on efficient assembly lines proved invaluable in fulfilling defense contracts in great volume, earning several Army–Navy Awards for Excellence. By war's end, Chris-Craft had delivered more than 10,000 landing craft, and their defense contract revenues had exceeded $20 million.

When Chris-Craft resumed production after World War II, the 20-foot Custom Runabout was the company's only truly new model. With bleached mahogany creating new deck patterns flowing right into the transom, the Custom provided a tantalizing glimpse of what might lie ahead for Chris-Craft enthusiasts. The Custom was the only Chris-Craft runabout to continue using the same folding windshield design created in 1941, and the 20-foot version offered from 1946 to 1949 is acknowledged as Chris-Craft's only advanced, totally new postwar design.

The shortages of mahogany immediately after World War II forced boat builders—trying desperately to fill orders for new models—to turn to such alternative woods as Spanish cedar. To compensate for the lack of suitable-grade mahogany, Chris-Craft's Special Runabouts and Racing Runabouts were available with painted hulls only. The new Riviera runabouts replaced the Customs in 1950, as mahogany once again became more abundant and the varnished hull was, again, the standard finish for Chris-Craft runabouts.

Automobile styling found its way into the Chris-Craft line-up in 1955, when the company introduced a boat they called the Cobra. Sporting a golden fiberglass dorsal tail fin, the single-cockpit sport craft, with its wraparound windshield, was offered as an 18-footer with speeds up to 39 miles per hour and a 21-footer with speeds of more than

Chris-Craft completely reorganized their line-up in 1955, placing their 19- and 21-foot models in the Capri series. This is a 21-foot model.

The 1955 Cobra, with its gold dorsal fin, was Chris-Craft's answer to the Chevrolet Corvette, which was introduced a year earlier. Produced for just one year, the 19- and 21-foot models are among today's most prized collectable runabouts.

The Capri series incorporated more automotive design elements than ever, as witnessed by its wraparound windshield and the dashboard styling shown here.

50 miles per hour. Not surprisingly, the Cobras drew large numbers of customers to dealer showrooms. However, in spite of all the attention, sales were so modest that production was discontinued after just one year. Thirty years later, those modest sales helped establish Cobras as some of the most desired classic runabouts among collectors.

The demand for new runabouts began to decline as boaters expressed greater preference for the roomier and more practical features of utility models. In 1961, Chris-Craft offered the last "pure" runabout model. In reality, the venerable utility progressed through several design transitions to become remarkably attractive and comfortable, with all the speed of the runabouts. These well-designed Sport Boats and Ski Boats were based on the typical utility configuration and are sometimes referred to as the next generation of runabouts. Today, the late-1960s models are often available at very reasonable prices to boaters craving the pleasures of an exciting mahogany sport boat. Most sport models are equipped with serviceable V-8 power, and provide a very practical (and affordable) way to experience classic boating for the first time.

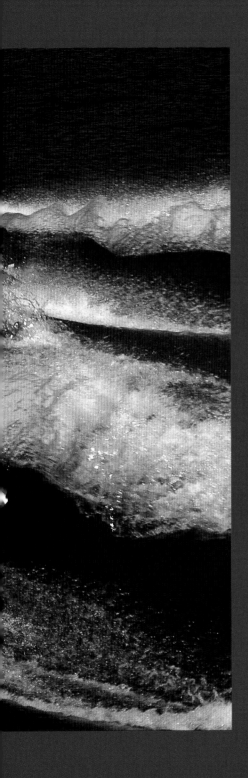

3

Watercars
Classics from the Dodge Auto Fortune

At the grand opening of the 1923 National Motor Boat Show in New York City, a brash young man from Detroit occupied a booth on the mezzanine floor to promote his new line of boats. Surprisingly, there were no boats displayed in his booth. He handed out hundreds of lavish brochures and boasted that his new factory would build boats from 16 to 120 feet in length. The enthusiastic, confident 23-year-old man was Horace Elgin Dodge, Jr., heir to a significant portion of the Dodge automobile fortune created by his father and uncle. His goal was to revolutionize recreational boating by building boats that put working-class families on the water, just as the Dodge brothers had helped put them in automobiles.

Shown here is an informal race between two Dodge runabouts. In the foreground is the Deluxe 1930 21-foot split-cockpit model with twin windshields. Behind is the 1936 19 1⁄2-foot model with dual cockpits forward. *Photo by Classic Boating Magazine*

Horace Dodge, Jr.'s first production Dodge Watercar was an attractive 22-footer with a long deck and a large aft cockpit. It was introduced at the 1924 National Motor Boat Show in New York City. *Photo by Classic Boating Magazine*

Horace always placed great value on the quality of his exhibit at the National Motor Boat Show, an important event for both the consumer and wholesale markets. For Dodge, it was an opportunity to take center stage and spin spirited messages to his dealers. In addition, the boat show was the traditional venue for dealers to place their orders for the new season—orders that guaranteed them spring delivery. More significantly, however, the orders determined the production volume goals that the factories would set for each model before laying off

workers. By the show's conclusion, virtually the entire year's production was determined.

Horace returned to the show in 1924, this time with a boat: his first production Dodge Watercar. The 22-foot sport runabout was powered by a 30-horsepower converted Dodge automobile engine located under a long deck, just forward of the cockpit. It was an attractive craft with a beautifully finished hull of African mahogany that would achieve 20 miles per hour. It was priced at $2,475 and was also available with a with a 90-horsepower government surplus

Curtiss V-8 aircraft engine. The converted Curtiss engines offered dependable power and speeds to 35 miles per hour for $2,975. Though modestly priced, the Watercars clearly missed the announced goal of creating an affordable boat for every family.

Dodge's initial marketing plan was to distribute his new Watercars through established Dodge automobile dealerships. To increase the publicity for his new enterprise, he also established a special motorboat race in honor of his father, offering the winner a trophy valued at more than $10,000.

With the new boat business underwritten by his family's fortune well under way, it was clear that Horace, who had nurtured a reputation for leading an irresponsible lifestyle, no longer had any interest in continuing with the automobile factory in any capacity. In December 1924, he brought significant credibility to his fledgling boat works by hiring George F. Crouch, the highly successful naval architect and race-boat designer, as the new firm's vice president. To join Dodge, Crouch left his position as professor of design at the prestigious Webb Institute of Long Island, New York, where he was recognized as one of the most creative new designers in powerboating. At Dodge, he was assigned full responsibility for designing all standardized Watercar models and establishing a system to assure quality control. In reality, it was probably more accurate that his

The cockpit of the early 22-foot Watercar is aft of the engine compartment, providing a large, roomy space with room for an additional wicker chair or two. *Photo by Classic Boating Magazine*

This early 22-foot Watercar, equipped with an optional Curtiss V-8 aircraft engine, achieved speeds up to 35 miles per hour. The standard engine was a 30-horsepower Dodge that produced a top speed of 20 miles per hour. *Photo by Classic Boating Magazine*

major responsibility was to design a series of racing boats to help Horace Dodge fulfill his dream of becoming Detroit's leading race-boat champion.

With Crouch assuming major responsibility, Horace continued his playboy ways, taking extended trips, drinking heavily, ignoring his faltering marriage, and giving little time to the boat business. It became clear to Crouch that Dodge's interest in personal pleasures far outweighed his passion for

building boats. Within two years, Crouch returned to New York, where he established an independent design firm. In 1927, after just six years of marriage, Dodge divorced his wife, and by 1928 the Dodge Boat Company had fallen into insolvency.

When Dodge announced that he planned to remarry and relocate to England, his furious mother, Anna, threatened to close the boat works permanently unless he returned to Detroit and assumed full responsibility for the operation. Though her ownership of the company was ostensibly to preserve her son's amateur race status, in reality she never felt Horace was responsible enough to hold such a post. Dodge, who was totally dependent on his mother for money, gave in and returned to Detroit. His mother refinanced the Dodge Boat Company and even sweetened the pie by letting Horace make plans for a new, enlarged factory in Newport News, Virginia. The new factory, the Horace E. Dodge Boat and Plane Corporation, was promoted as the world's largest pleasure-boat factory; Horace assured his mother that he would take full responsibility for managing the new facility and the anticipated work force of 2,000 employees.

In 1930, Dodge introduced a 16-foot runabout with fore and aft cockpits powered by a 40-horsepower Lycoming engine for $1,595. It became their all-time production leader. This boat is a 1932 model. *Photo by Classic Boating Magazine*

Beginning in 1930, the attractive nickel-silver sea nymph, shown on this 1932 16-foot runabout, adorned the bow of every Dodge runabout, a throwback to their proud automotive heritage. *Photo by Classic Boating Magazine*

With the introduction of the 1930 models, Dodge decided to drop the company's outmoded Watercar trademark. Still clinging to his association with Dodge automobiles, he commissioned a new trademark by Russell G. Crook, one of America's best-known sculptors. The graceful mermaid was cast in non-tarnishing nickel-steel and became standard on each Dodge runabout beginning in 1930. With construction of the Newport News

factory under way, Dodge announced that 157 authorized Dodge dealers were ready to sell the 1930 boats. He and Muriel Sisman, his new wife, celebrated his apparent success with a six-month trip around the world.

When news of the stock market collapse on October 29, 1929, reached Dodge, it appeared that his dream of building affordable boats for the common man would suffer another setback. Nonetheless, the new factory began production on March 13, 1930. But by then, the nation's economic depression had already become the controlling influence of the entire pleasure-boat industry, and sales continued to decline steadily through the 1933 season. Every marginal boat-building firm closed, while those able to hang on were running out of time. During the entire period, Horace managed only a few periodic visits to the struggling production lines in the new Virginia factory.

In spite of Dodge's undisciplined lifestyle, his vision for a quality, affordable craft was a worthy goal, and his association with one of America's leading naval architects, George Crouch, assured the development of attractively styled runabouts with solid performance potential. From 1924 until 1936, Dodge's boats challenged all competitors with fast, innovative styling and creative advertising campaigns. Ironically, the national economy was in recovery when Dodge production ceased in 1936. The closing of the Dodge plant at Newport News was a family decision reflecting a lack of interest in the business rather than any inherent failure of the boats.

The Dodge boat factory reopened for military production during World War II, producing naval assault boats. After the war, on February 22, 1946,

The 21 1/2-foot 1931 Dodge, with its 125-horsepower Lycoming engine and 35-mile-per-hour top speed, priced at $2,295, was the only production runabout to offer twin windshields on a two-cockpit model. *Photo by Classic Boating Magazine*

the factory's new owners announced that they had just negotiated a 10-year lease with Gar Wood Industries, which planned to build powerboats and light road-building machinery in Newport News for worldwide distribution. In another ironic twist, Horace Dodge again fell short in his lifelong quest to overtake his competitors, including Gar Wood, in racing and boat building.

True to his Gatsby-like lifestyle, Horace died in toney Grosse Pointe, Michigan, in 1963, of complications resulting from cirrhosis of the liver and heart disease. He was 63. No sooner was he laid to rest than a furor erupted over control of his estate. It seemed Horace Jr. had filed 11 wills over the course

of the previous 13 years, never anticipating that he would be outlived by his aged mother, nor that he would remain dependent on her for money. Within two months of his death, Anna Dodge filed a $10 million suit for loans she claimed to have made to her son. The probate judge remarked it had been "a long time since I have seen such a complicated and mixed-up family matter."

In 2001, only 68 Dodge boats were registered with the Antique and Classic Boat Society, an association that attracts the majority of active woodenboat owners. Although no production figures for Dodge boats are known to have survived, estimates range from 1,500 to as many as 2,500. (Comparing

The flagship of the 1930 Dodge fleet was this 28-foot runabout with its powerful 325-horsepower Lycoming engine.
Photo by Classic Boating Magazine

This attractive view of the 1931 21 1/2-foot Dodge runabout, with its gleaming African mahogany hull and sporty twin windshields, shows why it was such an appealing model. *Photo by Classic Boating Magazine*

the number of surviving wooden runabouts from similar boat builders, interpreting hull numbers, and gathering anecdotal information can provide fairly accurate estimates when no records are available.) Even these numbers seem modest in relation to Dodge's production capacity and the number of dealerships reported in their publications. However, it was not uncommon for boat builders to routinely exaggerate their production volume in advertisements and press releases.

4

Gar Wood
A Gentleman's Runabout

From the time he was a youngster, Gar Wood's commitment to speedboat racing seemed limitless. His creative genius resulted in several patented inventions, producing the abundant funds that made it possible for him to fulfill his dream to become the world's speedboat champion. He was so skilled at preparing, building, and driving race boats, he was virtually unbeatable for nearly two decades. He was also an avid outdoorsman who enjoyed cruising, sailing, fishing, hunting, and exploring remote areas of the Great Lakes in his high-speed cruisers, and a skilled airplane pilot who owned several aircraft built to his personal specifications. Whether on the water or in the air, Gar Wood's passion was speed.

Plenty of spray is what you can expect at 40 miles per hour in the cockpit of *Miss Behave*, the 1935 16-foot Gar Wood Speedster. *Courtesy Jim Brown*

Gar Wood was happy to concentrate on converting the vast number of surplus Liberty aircraft engines available after World War I for marine use. In fact, Gar Wood built the early 33-foot Baby Gar runabouts, including this 1927 model, primarily to demonstrate the remarkable performance of these powerplants in marine applications.

In 1922 Chris Smith and his sons left their partnership with Gar Wood to begin their own firm that later became the giant Chris-Craft. Wood helped finance the Smiths and commissioned the company to continue building Baby Gar runabouts for him in their new factory. The arrangement called for Smith to build the hulls and deliver them across town, where Wood's men installed their Gar Wood/Liberty engines.

It was a workable arrangement and Wood was happy to concentrate on converting the vast number of surplus Liberty aircraft engines stored in his warehouses to marine use. In fact, Gar Wood purchased thousands of the engines from the U.S. government at the conclusion of World War I and built the early 33-foot Baby Gar runabouts primarily to demonstrate the remarkable performance of the powerplants in marine applications.

After a short time, however, the Smiths increased production of their own boats, making it more difficult for them to deliver Baby Gars on schedule. Wood decided to solve the problem by building the hulls in his own shop.

In January 1930, Gar Wood completed construction of a new factory in Marysville, Michigan. Production of their 28-foot triple-cockpit runabout and a brand-new, 22-foot triple-cockpit runabout began on schedule. In addition, Gar Wood planned a totally new, flush-deck 33-foot runabout with a modern V-windshield as a replacement for the aging Baby Gar 33. The new 33-footer would be built in the old Algonac, Michigan, factory where Gar Wood still constructed custom and race boats. Everything was in place for a spectacular year. The

Gar Wood and custom runabout builders favored the superb 316-horsepower Scripps 302 V-12 engines with dual ignition, dual carburetors, and 894 ci of displacement. Beautiful to behold, this special marine engine was designed for smooth, responsive power and high-speed performance.

Buyers of big runabouts such as this 1927 33-foot Baby Gar often selected the option of a convertible canvas top to protect passengers from rain, spray, or chilly weather.

stock market crash of October 29, 1929, however, was beginning to take its toll on the nation's economy. For the first time ever, Gar Wood orders were canceled. Dealers were very cautious about ordering large, expensive runabouts without confirmed sales. As the national economy sank into a full-blown depression, orders for new Gar Woods slowed to a trickle and marginal boat builders were forced to close down.

But Gar Wood had a strong industrial empire to support his boat-building enterprise. He simply advised his key men in the boat shop to prepare designs for smaller, more affordable models that maintained Gar Wood's reputation for quality while keeping some production moving. In 1932 they introduced their first small runabout, an 18-foot model, with fore and aft cockpits, which sold for $1,200. It was followed by a smaller but no less attractive 16-foot model for $895. By 1935 the national economy was beginning to recover, but the small models, as well as practical utilities, had been so well received that boat builders were forced to re-evaluate their line-ups and provide acceptable alternatives to the powerful pre–Great Depression runabouts.

Perhaps the design most frequently associated with the name Gar Wood is the triple-cockpit runabout, a layout that provided two cockpits forward of the engine compartment and one smaller cockpit aft.

The 18-foot 1936 Gar Wood was the first model of this modest length to place both cockpits forward of the engine rather than one forward and one aft, as was customary up to that time.

Handsome 28-foot Gar Wood triple-cockpit runabouts, such as 1930s model, were the highest volume models built by Gar Wood from 1928 to 1941.

The famous 33-foot Baby Gar runabout built from 1922 to 1929 was Gar Wood's first example of this configuration. The triple-cockpit runabout was also offered in standard lengths of 28, 25, and 22 feet. These sleek, powerful craft became the toys of wealthy sportsmen from the 1920s to the start of World War II, and were luxuriously appointed with exquisite leather upholstery, an abundance of chrome trim, and attractive sport windshields. The larger models cost as much as the average three-bedroom American home, while the smaller versions were often more costly than the most luxurious automobiles of the time.

Wood's prized Liberty aircraft engines powered all of the early 33-foot Baby Gars. After his shop converted them for marine use, the powerplants were available in both 400- and 500-horsepower versions. Wood's highly skilled mechanics converted the powerful engines by the hundreds.

Gar Wood also offered runabouts with Scripps V-12s, strikingly beautiful engines that provided outstanding performance in a more compact package than the Liberty. The Scripps fit nicely into the 28-foot runabouts and even the 25-foot models. The 25-foot runabout, equipped with the Scripps V-12, rated at 300 horsepower, provided dependable performance and achieved speeds in the 50-mile-per-hour range. To be seated in the aft cockpit of one of these fabulous runabouts at high speed was a thrill nearly equivalent to flying in an open-cockpit airplane. Not surprisingly, rides in these spectacular triple-cockpit runabouts became popular forms of amusement at many lakeside communities.

As more people became interested in boating, builders diligently tried to create new models that were more affordable and still attractive. Boats that depended on inboard power have a minimum length. Gar Wood's limit was 16 feet. Their first 16-foot runabout was an offspring of the troubled economy and remained in the line-up through 1941, the same year that Wood sold his stock in the company. He remained connected with the company until the war's end, when he retired to his island estate in Florida. There, he continued to invent a range of products and design boats until his death in 1970 at age 90.

After World War II, an entirely new 16-footer was introduced as the price leader, a boat to help establish a much larger dealer organization. To qualify as a Gar Wood dealer, prospects were required to purchase a minimum of three new boats. The new 16-footer was modestly priced to help make the dealer's initial order reasonable and attractive. It was developed as an open utility rather than a runabout, which was the frequent choice for this length. The utility design offered more interior room and a low-maintenance painted hull and vinyl interior, resulting in wider appeal than the

These two thrill-seekers are about to take *Miss Behave*, a 16-foot 1935 Gar Wood Speedster, on a high-speed jaunt through the Thousand Islands region of upstate New York. *Courtesy Jim Brown*

runabout configuration. With three engine options that provided speeds up to 40 miles per hour, it turned out to be a remarkable craft that was a thrill to drive at top speeds.

In 1946, when Gar Wood Industries acquired the Horace E. Dodge Boat and Plane factory in Newport News, Virginia, the Boat Division decided that the facility, originally designed to produce small craft in large numbers, would be an excellent location to build the 16-foot utility. The boat was given the model name Ensign, and production began in July 1946. Between September 1946 and April 1947, the Newport News factory produced 550 Ensigns at a rate of more than 60 per month. They could have produced more if the operation had not been hampered by shortages of materials and marine engines. Today, the Ensign holds the distinction of being the model produced

Sixteen-foot Gar Wood Speedsters, such as *Miss Behave,* are capable of speeds over 50 miles per hour, requiring the helmsman's close attention. One of its most thrilling qualities is its absolutely level riding position at speed.
Courtesy Jim Brown

The aft cockpit of a big runabout is the perfect location for passengers to experience the excitement of the hull lifting from the surface under huge wings of spray.
Courtesy Dan Teetor

Gar Wood's 1946 and 1947 postwar models presented an interesting departure from earlier styling, with reverse sheer, rounded covering boards, barrel transoms, and barrel stems, as in this 19 1/2-foot Deluxe Runabout.
Courtesy Chris Johnson

Gar Wood's 17 1⁄2-foot 1946 runabout was the industry's only full-barrel back in the postwar field.

by Gar Wood in the highest volume, with a total of 650 built.

Gar Wood Industries' short-lived post–World War II fleet included two totally new runabout designs in 17 1/2-foot and 19 1/2-foot models. They also offered three utilities at 16, 18 1/2, and 22 1/2 feet; the latter two were also available as semi-enclosed models with attractive streamlined cabin enclosures. The postwar models were in production for just 13 months in both factory locations (Michigan and Virginia) with nearly 1,000 boats produced. It was the highest total volume in their history and a good indication of strong customer acceptance. Despite these record sales, Gar Wood's parent corporation decided to close the Boat Division abruptly and permanently in 1947. It was a sad and unexpected end to one of the greatest lines of runabouts and small craft in the golden era of mahogany boats.

5

John Hacker
Journeyman Builder and Designer

John Hacker influenced the design and performance of nearly every type, style, and length of powerboat for 60 years. As more efficient marine engines became available, weighing less and offering more power, Hacker grasped the opportunity to break from established designs. Hacker is also frequently credited as the most prolific and most successful marine designer of the first half of the twentieth century. In fact, he was responsible for more than 1,000 designs, ranging from dinghies to racing record-breakers to military air–sea rescue boats. Even today, many writers still refer to him as the dean of boat designers.

John Hacker began incorporating forward cockpits into his runabouts in 1920. The design shift came about after Edgar Gregory of the Belle Isle Boat and Engine Company finished four Hacker hulls to feature forward cockpits. The well-received departure stuck, as exhibited by this 1928 28-foot Hackercraft. *Photo by Classic Boating Magazine*

But John Hacker's passion and, indeed, his greatest talent was for the art and science of designing fast, distinctive craft. His creations were often on the cutting edge of achievement for pure beauty, remarkable speed, and outstanding performance. His novel approaches attracted clients who were willing to extend themselves in order to finance boats that took advantage of radical new concepts. Hacker, for example, was attracted to the early V-bottom hull designs and is even credited with building boats of this type while still a teenager. (Incredibly, he apparently continued to build a boat a year throughout his teen years.) When he discovered that he was able to achieve an additional 2 to 4 miles per hour using the V-bottom hull versus a traditional round-bottom hull of a similar size, he embraced the new design. Hacker's work on V-bottom designs and the parallel development of lighter, more powerful engines proved a winning combination, attracting great attention among buyers interested in gaining higher speeds.

In 1913, Hacker entered into a partnership with financier L. L. Tripp, who had the resources to finance a new boat-building enterprise. The new operation, called the Hacker Boat Company, was located on the Hudson River just north of Albany, New York. The goal of this new partnership was to build fast, high-quality boats of Hacker design. Hacker was enthusiastic and worked tirelessly to create a range of designs while supervising construction of each new boat. He also prepared designs for other boat companies, special clients, and boating magazines. The long hours eventually took their toll, and Hacker's health began to decline steadily to the point of a nervous breakdown. The designer was directed by his physician to stop working entirely and to take

John Hacker's passion and greatest talent were for the art and science of fast, distinctive craft, including race boats. *Meteor V,* a 1922 Hacker creation, was a Gold Cup racer. Rule changes instituted prior to that race season, intended to thwart Gar Wood's dominance of the sport, led to the emergence of the classic runabout that became the symbol of the golden era of beautiful mahogany-hulled boats. *Photo by Classic Boating Magazine*

an extended leave from the business. Reluctantly, he followed his doctor's advice, sold his share of the business to Tripp, and returned home to Detroit.

The company's name was changed to the Albany Boat Corporation and continued to actively promote Hacker's forward-cockpit runabouts. In 1917, Albany Boat Company modified the design slightly by installing the engine farther aft and using a gear drive to provide a large, single cockpit. The boat was sold to President Woodrow Wilson, bringing important recognition to the company and to Hacker, despite the tweaks to his original design.

After slowly regaining his health and re-establishing the Hacker Boat Company in Detroit, Hacker moved his operation to Mount Clemens, Michigan, where commercial waterfront property was more affordable.

About this time, Edgar Gregory of the Belle Isle Boat and Engine Company purchased four of Hacker's standardized 26-foot runabout hulls and installed a faster 125-horsepower Hall-Scott engine in each. Gregory purchased the four hulls without decking and finished them in his own

Apache, a fast 1926 Hackercraft 26-foot triple-cockpit runabout, demonstrates the advances John Hacker introduced with his designs. *Photo by Classic Boating Magazine*

The 1927 Hackercraft Dolphin was a very popular 24-foot, three-cockpit model with generous freeboard, a distinctive windshield, a high-crown deck, and Scripps power. *Photo by Classic Boating Magazine*

shop with a forward cockpit, the engine amidships, and a large aft cockpit. Gregory located the controls in the forward cockpit with the driver steering from a center position, ahead of the engine and clear of the boat's spray. It was a pleasant departure from driving the boat farther aft with hindered visibility. The forward cockpit idea and chic styling were well received and Gregory's runabouts became prototypes for the famous Belle Isle Bear Cats. The cockpit-forward style soon became the new standard for all runabouts.

Although Gregory was quick to take credit for every detail of the Bear Cat, and Hacker's larger custom runabouts began incorporating the cockpit-forward style in 1920, the runabout was still clearly a Hacker hull with Gregory's deck plan. Marine historian John Robinson reported in the January 1940 issue of *Motor Boating* magazine, "The Bear Cat was a sensation from the day it was launched." The Belle Isle Boat and Engine Company attained national prominence in the field, exhibiting at the New York Boat Show in 1920. In

The year 1929 represented a high water-mark throughout the wooden runabout industry. *Mahogany Magic* is a 30-foot, triple-cockpit Hackercraft from that year. *Photo by Classic Boating Magazine*

spite of the broad acceptance of the design, it was some time before many of the established boat builders embraced the advantage of this departure from traditional styling. Gregory continued this trend with a new 1922 runabout that featured two cockpits forward of the engine compartment and seating for four persons.

The following year Hacker presented his 21-foot Special to be marketed by Central Marine Services Corporation for $1,975, completely equipped and capable of 20 miles per hour. Hacker was beginning to understand the efficiency of producing standardized designs in larger volume. His old friend Henry Ford's company was the model for the

This 30-foot Hackercraft runabout from 1929 is powered by a 250-horsepower Sterling engine, providing excellent speed and a level ride. *Photo by Classic Boating Magazine*

economy of standardization, and Hacker believed that the same principle could be applied to boat building. To accomplish higher production volumes, Hacker began to specialize in a full line of standardized models that incorporated modern styling and the best features of the Bear Cat.

Orders for Hacker's standardized runabouts increased steadily right up until 1930; it was reported that deliveries peaked in June 1930 with a total of 90 boats. Nearly all boat builders were still enjoying the wake of 1929's record-setting boat sales, but the full impact of the Great Depression was just around the corner. In 1934 John Hacker turned over his financial interest in the Hacker Boat Company to young Mac McCready and McCready's father, who had been a part owner

since 1925. Hacker returned to Detroit, where he turned his full attention to design work. He agreed to continue designing boats for the Hacker Boat Company from his modest Detroit studio.

After 1934 John Hacker, the designer, and the Hacker Boat Company, builders of Hackercraft boats, were separate entities. Over the years, the company continued to contract with Hacker and their relationship remained amicable. Largely as a result of that genial partnership, the Hacker Boat Company was able to work its way through the grim years of the depression. By 1935 the boat business was in recovery and Hackercraft unveiled a 17-foot utility that retailed for $975. The following six years marked a steady return to pre–Great Depression production levels.

In the early-1920s John Hacker began to understand the significance of standardized designs as pioneered by his old pal, Henry Ford. Compare this relatively Spartan Hacker dashboard with the Gar Wood instrument panel on page 12. *Photo by Classic Boating Magazine*

In the late 1930s the U.S. Department of the Army asked John Hacker and Gar Wood to submit designs for fast military craft that could provide shore gunners with experience shooting at moving targets. The boats needed to be capable of moving various targets at high speed to simulate battle conditions. In addition, the craft obviously needed to be able to operate without a driver, using a remote-control system. Both designs were accepted and an equal number of each type was ordered for immediate construction.

The two designs differed significantly in style. Gar Wood's boat had a typical "all business" military appearance, while Hacker's target boat presented an attractive profile with a swept windshield, rounded covering boards, a barrel bow, and a nicely raked transom. It met all the military requirements and still looked exciting. Even a military work boat provided Hacker with an opportunity to incorporate his flair for attractive design principles. In fact, one of Hacker's most noteworthy designs, the 48-foot runabout *Pardon Me,* incorporates many of the design

Previous pages: It was reported that deliveries of Hacker's standardized runabouts peaked in June 1930 with a total of 90 boats—clearly, the full gravity of the depression was yet to be realized. Both of these Hackercraft are from that model year—a 28-footer at top, and a 30-foot model at bottom. *Photo by Classic Boating Magazine*

Above: Some argue that Hacker's design skills culminated not with his runabouts but with *Thunderbird,* a 55-foot commuter built in 1939 for a real estate magnate who owned a lodge on Lake Tahoe. *Photo by Classic Boating Magazine*

Below: John Hacker's gift for engineering distinctive performance and a smooth ride are apparent in this photo of his 1936 24-foot runabout. *Photo by Classic Boating Magazine*

Above: By 1952, this marvelous 25 1/2-foot Hackercraft was among the last of the big, standardized triple-cockpit models from the traditional runabout builders. Powered by the Scripps V-12, it reached 48 miles per hour and held up to 11 passengers.

In 1933, this 32-foot, 14-passenger custom runabout became one of John Hacker's outstanding contributions to powerboating. Driven by a 12-cylinder, 450-horsepower Kermath Sea Raider, the remarkable boat effortlessly reached speeds of 55 miles per hour.

elements that Hacker used on his target boat. Built just after World War II by the Hutchinson Boat Works in Alexandria Bay, New York, this magnificent boat, now on exhibit at the Antique Boat Museum in Clayton, New York, is powered by an 1,800-horsepower Packard V-12 engine and is claimed to be the world's largest runabout.

With the onset of World War II, Hackercraft was assigned a series of important defense contracts for target boats and Navy picket boats. At war's end, Hacker returned to runabout and utility production. But because so many government contractors decided to enter the pleasure-boat market, competition was severe. The traditional Hacker style was no longer in demand and their old market for high-class custom runabouts was virtually gone.

6

Sea-Lyon
Timing Is Everything

Howard Lyon was a dapper, well-connected New Yorker with exceptional promotional capabilities. He was also confident enough to believe that he could achieve whatever he focused his mind on. In 1926 Lyon used his power of persuasion to convince the ever-cautious Gar Wood that he could sell boats as quickly as Wood's Algonac shop could build them. When Lyon sold expensive 33-foot Baby Gars in record numbers to many prominent American and foreign sportsmen, Gar Wood was impressed and agreed to grant Lyon an exclusive arrangement to sell his runabouts.

In the late 1920s, Howard Lyon's 30-foot Sea-Lyon runabouts took dead aim at Gar Wood's hold on the upper end of the runabout market. This 1930 Sea-Lyon Model 45 runabout was designed by Ned Purdy and is powered by its original 225-horsepower Sterling Petrel engine. It is one of the few surviving Sea-Lyons. *Photo by Classic Boating Magazine*

Howard Lyon became a Hackercraft dealer after parting company with Gar Wood. This 1928 Sea-Lyon 26-foot runabout was designed by John Hacker and built at the Hackercraft plant in Michigan. *Courtesy Jack Savage*

Lyon opened a plush showroom at the Barclay Hotel in midtown Manhattan. From this prestigious location, he sold Baby Gar runabouts to prominent businessmen and international heads of state. He followed each of these sales successes with attractive display ads listing the names of the men with the obvious good taste to buy Baby Gars. Lyon even convinced many of Gar Wood's engine, paint, tool, hardware, and lumber suppliers to sponsor major display ads promoting their involvement with Gar Wood boats and his dealership. As a result, Gar Wood's modest factory in Algonac couldn't produce boats fast enough to satisfy his new national distributor.

In spite of his sales accomplishments, Lyon was frequently at odds with Wood over a variety of suggestions. Lyon prepared lists of changes he felt certain would improve the marketability of the boats. He repeatedly requested special modifications to the standardized boats and promised customers unworkable delivery dates. Lyon's aggressive style became a source of stress for Wood. For his part, Lyon perceived that little was being done to increase production or to make the changes that he deemed necessary. In the fall of 1927, Lyon began to investigate the feasibility of building his own line of boats that would incorporate the best features of Gar Wood boats and the changes he felt would improve their marketability. It didn't take long for news about Lyon's lofty plans to get back to Gar Wood. Not surprisingly, the highly successful distribution arrangement between Lyon and Wood was terminated.

Lyon was confident that his own fleet of runabouts could become a major force in the world's exploding runabout market. As a stop-gap measure

Howard Lyon's marketing skills, location, confidence, and attractive boats all seemed to assure him of enormous success as he launched his new enterprise. In 1929, the model year of this double-cockpit model, Sea-Lyon was sourcing six powerplants from six manufacturers. *Photo by Classic Boating Magazine*

A handsome instrument panel and unique five-section windshield, with its pivoting center section for flow-through ventilation, were trademarks of Sea-Lyon runabouts. *Photo by Classic Boating Magazine*

to hold him over until his boats became reality, Lyon became Hackercraft's exclusive East Coast distributor, and arranged for custom boat builder Ned Purdy to prepare additional runabout designs. Lyon also secured the financial backing to carry out his program swiftly, without losing the sales momentum he created selling Gar Wood boats, and purchased the Kyle & Purdy Shipyard in City Island, New York, as a facility in which to build and service his new boats. With 300 feet of waterfront and outside storage for 100 large cruisers and yachts, the shipyard was one of the largest and most complete yacht yards in the New York City area. Inside, there was enough space to store 150

runabouts. The new partnership would be called the Lyon-Tuttle Corporation, named for Lyon and an investor.

The early 26-foot Sea-Lyon runabouts and sedans were designed and built by the Hacker Boat Company in Mount Clemens, Michigan, and remained in their offerings through 1928. In 1929, just two years into the operation, Sea-Lyon offered six stock runabouts, each with a list of options:

· 24-foot Sea-Lyon 30 with a 75-horsepower Chrysler Crown, $2,675
· 24-foot Sea-Lyon 35 with a 120-horsepower Chrysler Imperial, $2,975

- 28-foot Sea-Lyon 40 with a 225-horsepower Kermath or 200-horsepower Scripps, $4,650
- 30-foot Sea-Lyon 45 with a 200-horsepower Sterling Petrel, $5,950
- 30-foot Sea-Lyon 46 with a 200-horsepower Sterling Petrel, $6,500
- 30-foot Sea-Lyon 50 with a 300-horsepower Hall-Scott, $8,000

Much of Lyon's advertising, including his elaborate sales brochures, emphasized the important differences between Sea-Lyon runabouts and those of competitors. In many ways, the differences listed in Sea-Lyon sales literature appeared directed at Gar Wood boats, though they did not identify any particular builder. Howard Lyon's most important market was the New York metropolitan area and Long Island Sound. An early brochure stated:

> From the first, our purpose has been to build not merely more boats, but better boats suited to coastal waters to meet the exacting demands of Eastern yachtsmen.

Sea-Lyons were designed to be high-quality versions of the best standard runabouts that first achieved popularity in the late 1920s. The Honduran mahogany selected for the hull and deck planking was fractionally thicker than that of the competition's mahogany. This is a 30-foot model from 1930.

With its long fore deck and five-sectioned windshield, the 30-foot Sea-Lyon runabout was an impressive craft that provided a remarkably smooth ride. *Photo by Classic Boating Magazine*

Until the advent of the Sea-Lyon, there was not even one prominent make of runabout built on salt water.

When the sales brochures pointed out that every illustration was an actual photo, it was in reference to builders who airbrushed studio photos to simulate water and spray and make the boats appear as if they were operating at speed.

Interestingly, Sea-Lyon brochures also explained how their boats compensated for the excessive torque that caused fast runabouts—often large Chris-Craft and Gar Wood models—to list to one side when running at speed:

In Sea-Lyons torque is compensated perfectly by building the hull bottom on one side slightly different from the other side so that there is no list from this cause, either when running or at rest. . . . In other runabouts we have found this torque effect is partially concealed but not really compensated by such devices as ballasting one side more than the other, or even by painting the waterline incorrectly.

Howard Lyon's decision to create his own fleet of standardized runabouts was a bold move motivated both by his unprecedented success as a Gar Wood dealer and the belief that his improvements would be so effective that buyers would be drawn to his boats. His marketing strategy was superb and his boats were excellent products, priced appropriately in relation to the market. His Manhattan showroom and City Island boatyard seemed a strong combination. In addition, the eastern market appeared lucrative and

Capable of impressive speeds, the 30-foot Sea-Lyon featured a level-riding hull that provided excellent visibility in spite of the long fore deck. *Photo by Classic Boating Magazine*

used. Additionally, Sea-Lyon windshields were styled with a pivoting center section for ventilation, plus double side wings to provide additional protection. The large engine hatches were built in four sections rather than the customary two units, and all cockpit and engine room flooring was made in easy-to-remove sections to provide quick access to the bilge. All of these improvements were impressive and came directly from the list of ideas that Lyon had wanted Gar Wood to incorporate during their association. His approach was convincing and buyers seemed impressed.

But the stock market crash and ensuing economic depression were fatal events for the fledgling operation. Everything Lyon accomplished was the result of self-confidence and boundless energy. While assuring himself that he could maintain his operation until the inevitable recovery, Lyon did everything he could to continue marketing his boats, hold off creditors, and reduce prices. But eventually there was nothing left he could do and in 1932 his heroic assault on Michigan runabout builders ended forever in a New York City courtroom. His dream of the great eastern runabout factory finally vanished. The personal loss was devastating and Lyon would never resurrect his vision.

The original Sea-Lyon factory data and production records apparently have not survived. As a result, it's difficult to estimate accurately their total

Expressly designed to be high-quality versions of the best standard runabouts of the time, Sea-Lyons featured Honduran mahogany hull and deck planking that was fractionally thicker than the competition's. A piece of specially selected white oak was used for the full length of the keel. *Photo by Classic Boating Magazine*

ready for Lyon's classy runabouts. As with Lyon's old Gar Wood ads, his Sea-Lyon advertisements proudly included updated lists of the well-known purchasers. The new Sea-Lyon owner's list included such names as William Vanderbilt, helicopter pioneer Igor Sikorsky, Edward Noble of the Life Saver candy fortune, tire manufacturer David Goodrich, racing champion Caleb Bragg, automobile magnate Powel Crosley, Cadillac figure Lawrence Fisher, and others. In several cases, these were the same people who had previously purchased Gar Wood boats from Lyon. Clearly, Lyon targeted many of his former Gar Wood customers with attractive trade-in offers. As a result, Sea-Lyon ads often created the impression that Gar Wood owners were eager to swap their old boats for new Sea-Lyons. Lyon's marketing skills, location, confidence, and attractive boats all seemed to assure him of several years of enormous success as he launched his new enterprise into the boating world in 1929.

Sea-Lyon boats were expressly designed to be high-quality versions of the best standard runabouts that first achieved popularity in the late

The 30-foot Sea-Lyon runabout was expressly designed for the wave conditions normally experienced in Long Island Sound. *Photo by Classic Boating Magazine*

Despite the impressive performance and design of Howard Lyon's boats, the stock market crash and ensuing Great Depression proved fatal for the fledgling operation. *Photo by Classic Boating Magazine*

1920s. The Honduran mahogany selected for the hull and deck planking was fractionally thicker than that of the competition. One piece of specially selected white oak was used for the full length of the keel and for the chines. Step-pad frames were carefully designed to provide a nearly level surface for additional safety. All deck fittings and hardware castings were made of nickel silver to avoid the possibility of peeling or corroding. Even fine details such as hidden fastenings for deck hardware were

production volume by model, though their sales were concentrated primarily in the Northeast and New York City. Today, they are rare and considered highly collectable by enthusiasts.

Sea-Lyons were quality runabouts that deserved a better fate. Introducing a fleet of large, powerful, luxury runabouts in late 1928 was a prime example of bad timing that overwhelmed quality, aesthetics, and superior performance. In this case, timing was everything.

7

Lyman
The Secure Performer

Bernard Lyman was just 11 when his family emigrated from Prussia to America in 1861. As a young man in Cleveland, Ohio, he developed into a skilled cabinetmaker and opened his own shop. On the side, Lyman enjoyed building distinctive lapstrake fishing boats for his personal use. Traditional lapstrake hull construction was somewhat uncommon on small boats in the region, and friends admired the small fishing boats so much they bought each one Lyman built.

Lyman's boats, which began to gain modest fame in the region, were well suited not only for fishing, but also for the scores of rental liveries on the shores of Lake Erie. Lyman observed that these operations always seemed to be in need of new boats, either to replace old ones or to expand their fleets. Since rental companies in the Cleveland area did not have a good local source, Lyman was convinced that their demand represented a sound business opportunity. Gradually, he decided that building small boats might be more fulfilling, both financially and artistically, than cabinetmaking, and in 1875 he opened a small shop to make watercraft.

This solidly built 1967 Lyman 19-foot runabout offers a generous beam of over 7 feet, a massive windshield, and a 35-mile-per-hour top speed with its 165-horsepower engine. *Photo by Classic Boating Magazine*

The Lyman Boat Works created a huge following of devoted enthusiasts with their outstanding outboard models, such as this staunch 15-footer. When Lyman owners moved up to inboard runabouts, they nearly always remained loyal to Lyman.

Lyman's boat business grew steadily through the years following World War I, and in 1928 his son William ("Bill") took over management of the enterprise. With his and his father's experience building a variety of sizes and types, young Lyman felt comfortable building both outboard and small inboard models. When Bernard Lyman died in 1934 at age 84, his son was fully involved in every phase of the family business, and within a short time Bill decided to move it farther west along Lake Erie to Sandusky, Ohio. He was confident that the change in location would ultimately provide a more secure future and better potential for expansion.

Lyman boats, with their round-bottom, clinker-built lapstrake hulls, were ideally suited for large, choppy bodies of water such as Lake Erie. So Bill Lyman continued to focus on building boats for practical boaters who liked to fish and hunt and needed the security of a rugged craft. In addition, Lyman provided his boats with adequate space for tackle and equipment, and ensured the craft were easy to maintain. He also realized that the sportsmen attracted to his boats needed models that were modestly priced. He was convinced that this could become Lyman's special niche in the boating market.

Bill Lyman was very proud of the boats and described their unique hull construction method this way:

Lapstrake or clinker-built hulls date back eight centuries or more to the early Scandinavian voyagers. This type of construction had very definite advantages then, which still hold today. Fundamentally, lapstrake

Lyman identified many of their models as runabouts, despite their resemblance to the utility boats of other manufacturers. This 1952 19-foot lapstrake "runabout" achieved speeds up to 35 miles per hour. *Photo by Classic Boating Magazine*

construction implies the assembly of individual planks or strakes over a rib cage framework with a stem-keel backbone and a transom terminating board. These strakes are overlapped on each other and fastened to each other as well as to the ribs or frames, stem-keel and transom.

Lyman established guidelines to enhance his distinction as a boat builder. The foremost goal was to develop soft-riding, sea-kindly lapstrake hulls of clinker construction. In addition, consistent design elements among different lengths and models would keep construction costs modest. Shortly after the 1929 stock market crash, Lyman developed a 17-foot inboard model with its engine located in a box rather than the usual large compartment. Some authorities consider this the first production utility model. The arrangement proved ideal and became their standard inboard design for all models, eventually evolving

Lyman's 1954 18-foot runabout resembled their Islander model. However, the 18-footer was faster, featured forward controls and automotive steering, and provided a level-riding hull that was fun to drive at speed.

into an attractive, sensible boat with a highly recognizable appearance. Lyman's guidelines had resulted in a formula for success, even through the lean depression years. Lyman soon offered cabin enclosures as a practical option for larger inboard models, and occasionally built small or mid-size cabin cruisers on special order.

The Lyman Boat Works was one of the first private boat builders to be issued defense contracts shortly after the Japanese attacked Pearl Harbor on December 7, 1941. The government contracts issued to Lyman specified five different types of boats to be supplied to the Navy, the Corps of Engineers, and

the Army Air Force. Lyman did such an exemplary job filling each of their defense contracts that the company was officially recognized with the Army–Navy Award for Excellence. But perhaps their most valuable reward was the experience gained developing greater production efficiency to meet the rigid deadlines specified in the government contracts. During the war, hulls were constructed on modified assembly lines that required skilled labor only for the original set-up of the molds and jigs. The approach worked so well that it became standard operating procedure in the early postwar boom years, even though the size of their facilities restricted the number of assembly lines that could be established. As a result, production was limited to three outboard models, one rowboat, one combination rowing and outboard hull, and the 18-foot inboard Islander runabout.

The wartime use of marine plywood also opened Lyman's eyes to its greater strength and weight advantages over traditional solid planking. Prewar Lymans were constructed with white oak frames and planking of Philippine mahogany or, in some cases, vertical-grain tidewater cypress. After the war, white oak frames were still used, but the company decided to plank their postwar hulls with high-grade fir plywood. Plywood provided another benefit over solid mahogany, namely its ready availability.

Bill Lyman was absolutely convinced from the outset that plywood was ideal for their clinker-built planking method, stating, "Marine grade plywood . . . because it is always uniform, does not alternately swell and contract and lends itself to a perfect bond where plank meets plank." The plywood was not used in sheets, but was cut into planks and handled as if it were conventional lumber. In a brochure, the Lyman Boat Works described how their hulls were constructed:

The 1958 19-foot Lyman runabout gained considerable attention, even though it shared many features with the earlier 18-foot model.

In 1962, the 20-foot Lyman runabout took on the company's new larger boat appearance, with a beam of 7 feet, 8 inches; plenty of cockpit room; and a hull that could handle rough seas.

A Lyman hull begins upside down with a white oak stem-keel over an exact mold form to which is fastened a mahogany plywood transom. Steam formed white oak ribs or frames are spaced 6" to 7" apart are then molded into place. These ribs are full length from gunwale to gunwale with the exception of a few in the bow area which are mortised to the stem-keel. Contoured marine plywood planks (or strakes) are then fastened in place . . . with silicon bronze screws.

During the early postwar years, Lyman quickly realized that the market for outboard boats was going to be very strong. This suited the company perfectly since these models were not held up waiting for outsourced components and could be shipped as quickly as they were produced. Their 13-foot and 15-foot outboard models were shipped as quickly as they were built. During this time, Lyman also realized that it was much easier to establish new dealerships for outboard boats than it was for inboard models; service stations, used-car dealers, sporting good retailers, and even hardware stores were eager to become first-time outboard boat dealers.

Although the first postwar Lyman brochures included 18- and 22-foot inboard models, a short supply of marine engines (caused by a heavy demand for automobiles) and the popularity of outboard models reduced the need to build the larger runabouts. Outboard boats were shipped to the new network of dealers as soon as the last coat of paint had dried. Lyman kept outboard production moving at peak levels while building the inboard Islander utility only when they were assured of engine deliveries.

The abundant supply of marine plywood gave Lyman a special advantage in this area as well. Chris-Craft, Gar Wood, Century, Hackercraft, and others depended on well-seasoned mahogany and struggled to find it. Lyman production, meanwhile, remained steady, much to the delight of their rapidly growing dealer network.

Over the next six years, Lyman's production-line system was refined so that by 1951 they were turning out a completed outboard hull every 35 minutes and a finished inboard boat every 7 hours. Their production was outstanding, not only in quantity but in quality, as well. Production volume for 1951 reached nearly 4,000 units. In 1952, just as Lyman was experiencing ever-increasing production and success, Bill Lyman died at age 69. His death ended nearly 80 years of exclusive father-and-son management. Fred Wiehn, who served as corporate vice president and knew the business extremely well, became Lyman's new president, with little disruption to the operation.

The 1965 Lyman 19-foot runabout showed increased hull flair, a massive windshield frame, and a wider beam, as Lyman went head-to-head with Chris-Craft's new Sea Skiffs.

The 21-foot Lyman runabout in 1963 clearly demonstrated the well-established Lyman image with forward flair, substantial beam, a massive windshield, and the characteristic Lyman stem profile.

By 1958 the factory had a staff of 185 employees and increased their annual production volume to 5,000 boats, their peak year. The two models identified as runabouts that year were 19- and 23-foot boats providing speeds up to 36 miles per hour.

As Lyman entered the 1960s, greater emphasis was placed on building inboard models, a response to market changes and the desire of outboard owners to move up to larger craft. Chris-Craft's new Sea Skiff Division, with their well-publicized line of "round bilge lapstrake models," quickly became a formidable competitor for Lyman customers. In 1962, Lyman responded by increasing the lengths of their runabouts from 19 to 20 feet and making their 23-footer a 24-footer. Lyman also dropped the term "runabout" for the 24-footer, identifying it

instead as the "Sleeper," in reference to the V-berths beneath its wide forward deck.

As their inboard fleet gained wider recognition and faced increased competition from Century, Chris-Craft, and even Cruis-a-long, Lyman responded with a series of styling improvements. Their wooden hulls began featuring additional flair and attractive contours to accompany exceptional performance, and their lapstrake construction approached perfection in style and integrity. By the mid-1960s, Lyman was offering runabouts in 19 and 21 feet before dropping the term in describing their smaller inboards in advertising material.

Lyman boats were safe, secure, and conservative, and their segment of the market was so assured that they were caught by surprise when

Century, Chris-Craft, and others invaded their domain with nearly identical designs. It appears that Lyman had never anticipated the possibility and by the time they expanded their offerings, Chris-Craft had taken over the round bilge, lapstrake market. Lyman responded with excellent models, but never completely recovered. They were also slow to recognize the inevitable conversion to fiberglass construction and stubbornly resisted adapting. When totally new fiberglass designs were introduced, they were disappointing. Almost overnight it became apparent that the end of this distinguished, longstanding firm was quickly closing in.

There are still many regions where serious sportsmen prefer 50-year-old Lymans, with their superior wooden lapstrake construction, to fiberglass boats of the same size. In some areas, veteran fishing guides even use their vintage wooden Lymans to treat clients to a day's fishing. Currently, the survival rate of vintage Lyman wooden hulls is among the highest of all their contemporary builders. And although many Lymans participate in classic boat shows, most are still providing outstanding service in their intended roles as desirable sport craft, a true testament to Bernard Lyman's formula for success.

Although this big 24 1/2-foot Lyman could sleep two under the large fore deck, the company still classified it as a runabout in their brochures and advertising campaigns.

8

Century
Speed, Style, and Creativity

The Century Boat Company was the dream of two brothers, William and James Welch, who started their boat-building enterprise in Milwaukee in 1926. Their goal at the outset was to build a line of small, standardized boats for outboard power and to gain national recognition by developing one or two outboard race boats. As the outboard motor industry developed, enthusiasm for speed and racing grew rapidly, and the Welch brothers saw the craze as an opportunity to promote their standard models. By 1929, the new company had an impressive fleet of mahogany boats, including the 13 1/2-foot Kid, the 15 1/2-foot Traveler Jr., the 17-foot Traveler, and the Sea King and Seadan, both 19-footers. In addition, the Welches also offered the Cyclone, a race-only model.

The stylish blonde and dark mahogany deck pattern, such as that on *Lynn Anne*, a beautiful 17 1⁄2-foot 1947 Century Sea Maid, delighted buyers looking for refreshing postwar innovations. *Photo by Classic Boating Magazine*

In the early 1930s, the Century Thunderbolt runabout started a trend among standardized production boat builders: single-cockpit sport racers. *Photo by Classic Boating Magazine*

The Welch brothers had lofty expectations for their first four years in business and, in spite of their impressive line-up, sales fell short of their goals. Part of the problem was the Milwaukee facility's limited production capacity. After four years in Milwaukee, they decided to relocate their operation to Manistee, Michigan, on the opposite shore of Lake Michigan. The new location appeared more suitable for building and marketing their new boats. As luck would have it, the move took place just before the October stock market crash in 1929.

But the cost of relocating and setting up new production systems in the midst of the Great Depression was more than the brothers could handle. As the depression dragged on, the Welches sold their business to a Detroit group seeking a promising investment opportunity. The new owners, the son of prominent naval architect John Hacker among them, continued to operate the business under the established Century Boat Company name and moved quickly to promote speed as an inherent feature of their boats.

In early spring 1931, a stock Century Thunderbolt runabout was entered in the new 125 Class of the prestigious 142-mile Albany-to-New York Outboard Marathon Race, which it won by 40 minutes with an average speed of 41 miles per hour. As if that weren't impressive enough, several Century outboard models won or placed in other classes. It turned out to be a publicity coup.

As various new class designations encouraged wider participation, interest in outboard racing continued to grow. Century's new color catalog was spectacular and introduced several exciting outboard hydroplanes with such model names as Cyclone, Hurricane, and Black Demon. The moniker Sea Maid was given to their 17-foot inboard runabout, a dual forward-cockpit design that continued for several years. The attractive Sea Maid featured a radical planking technique in which the outside edge of each bottom plank overlapped the inside edge of the plank above it. It was simply a form of lapstrake construction reserved just for the bottom planks; the lap pattern, however, was reversed from the traditional method, providing a stiffer bottom, slightly less wetted surface, and better directional tracking. Century used the same-style bottom on their 14-foot Thunderbolt inboard racing runabout and the 16-foot split-cockpit runabout, promoting it as the "Air Cushion Bottom" in reference to the gaps between the lapped bottom planks and the framing. During this same period, John Hacker left his

Century offered this sporty 15-foot Sea Maid runabout in 1940, with fore and aft cockpits and speeds up to 36 miles per hour.

boat-building firm for independent design work and is reported to have contributed Century's early runabout designs.

From a creative standpoint, Century's dual forward-cockpit runabout and their single aft-cockpit racing runabout were well ahead of two formidable and well-established contemporary runabout builders. Both the Thunderbolt and Sea Maid preceded Gar Wood's famous Speedster (1934) and dual-cockpit forward runabout (1936), as well as Chris-Craft's 16-foot Racing Hydroplane (1936) and 18-foot dual forward-cockpit runabout (1934). The two Century runabouts moved the boat builder into the fast lane and served notice that it was both innovative and motivated to become a major player in the runabout market.

Century continued to focus their creativity on small runabouts, utilities, sedans, and a few outboard models, a range with which they were comfortable. Century also decided to concentrate

This compact 1942 Century triple-cockpit Sea Maid, *Sweet Louise*, houses a 140-horsepower Gray Fireball engine. *Photo by Classic Boating Magazine*

exclusively on single-plank bottom construction, supporting their decision with official statements:

Single-planked boat bottoms are just as strong as double-planked bottoms, inasmuch as heavier planking is used on the former. Single-planking of thickness comparable to double-planking will stand just as great shock of impact, and will last just as many years with the same kind of care.

Almost any boat owner with a few simple tools can easily repair a break or leak in a single-planked bottom, while the services of a boat carpenter are usually required to repair a double-planked bottom. Another advantage of single-planking is the fact that there is less tendency to buckling. When water penetrates between double-planking, an expensive repair job is a virtual certainty.

Finally, a novice may easily locate any leak in single-planked bottoms, while it is often impossible even for an expert to locate a leak in double-planked construction without removing much of the planking.

Contemporary boat restorers confirm that single-plank bottoms are much easier to repair than traditional canvas-covered double-plank bottoms. However, they also point out that double-plank bottoms were superior in construction and nearly leak-proof.

Century's 1940 runabout fleet was launched with their 15-foot Sea Maid split-cockpit model that reached 36 miles per hour with its 62-horsepower Gray Phantom Four. Seventeen-foot Sea Maid runabouts offered two deck plans on the same hull. The fore and aft cockpit version featured four engine options with speeds up to a remarkable 52 miles per hour, thanks to a Gray Racing Fireball or a Lycoming Racing Six. It was an impressive feat for a production runabout in 1940. It was also a glimpse into the sort of high-speed performance that Century enjoyed offering their devoted customers. The other version of the Sea Maid 17 was the twin cockpit-forward model offered with the Gray Phantom Four in 62-horsepower and 81-horsepower options, with a top speed of 35 miles per hour.

In 1940, Century also offered an 18 1/2-foot Sea Maid runabout available in three seating configurations. The double-cockpit models were available with fore and aft cockpits and with dual forward cockpits. Similar to the dual cockpit-forward model, the fore and aft cockpit boat was available with four engine

With their 1942 line-up, Century continued to show the boating industry that three cockpits could be wedged into a 20-foot Sea Maid runabout. *Photo by Classic Boating Magazine*

options up to the 140-horsepower Gray Fireball that produced speeds as high as 42 miles per hour. Century also presented their 18 1/2-foot Sea Maid hull in a triple-cockpit model with speeds to 35 miles per hour produced by the 103-horsepower Gray Phantom Six. Century's premier Sea Maid, however, was a 20-foot triple-cockpit runabout with three engine options reaching speeds of 40 miles per hour with the 140-horsepower Gray Fireball.

All of these 1940 Sea Maids were equipped with "the sensationally new, crystal-clear, unbreakable, curved Plexiglas windshields," as described in the manufacturer's catalog that year. Additionally, the 17-, 18-, and 20-foot Sea Maids featured the new streamlined, winged bowplate that provided a

barrel-bow look to the top of the stem. Standard upholstery was high-quality Naugahyde in four color options. Leather upholstery was available for an additional $42 for two cockpits and $65 for triple-cockpit models.

In 1941, the 15-foot Sea Maid was increased in length to 16 feet. The resulting line-up remained essentially the same until all pleasure-boat production ceased in early 1942, when Century became a successful defense contractor, earning the coveted Army–Navy Award for Excellence and exceeding the armed forces' rigid requirements for assault boats.

At war's end, Century announced three new Sea Maid runabouts in the 1946 National Motor

The earliest postwar Century runabout was the 1946 15-foot Sea Maid with split cockpits. It was identical to Century's final prewar 15-foot production Sea Maid, and Century's last split-cockpit model to locate both cockpits forward of the engine compartment. *Photo by Classic Boating Magazine*

Boat Show issue of *Motor Boating* magazine. The anticipated new models were a 15-footer, a 17 1/2-footer, and a 19-footer.

By the time Century made the transition from defense work to peacetime production in mid-1947, there were only two Sea Maids in production: the 17 1/2-footer and the 19-footer. Both presented a new postwar look with an attractive deck pattern of blonde and red mahogany complemented by cockpit upholstery that continued the pattern. Speed and detailing were clearly emerging as the distinguishing characteristics of Century boats, and with Gar Wood's Boat Division closing permanently at the same time, Century was Chris-Craft's most significant rival for control of the exciting runabout market.

In 1950 the phrase "Thoroughbred of Boats," accompanied by the silhouette of a rearing horse,

The 1948 Sea Maid 19-footer, with its beautifully styled two-tone deck coloration, luxurious upholstery, and blazing speed was one of the most popular runabouts of the year. *Photo by* **Classic Boating** *Magazine*

As speed and detailing clearly emerged as the distinguishing characteristics of Century boats—and with Gar Wood's parent company closing the Boat Division permanently at the same time—Century, with models such as this 1951 Resorter, became Chris-Craft's most significant rival. *Photo by Classic Boating Magazine*

In 1959, the Century Boat Company became a subsidiary of the Overlakes Corporation. The change was nothing new to longtime employees, as ownership changes at Century had occurred with far greater frequency than at any other of the major builders of popular runabouts. Dodge, Chris-Craft, Gar Wood, Lyman, Higgins, and Sea-Lyon had all operated under a single owner. Hackercraft was transferred just once. In addition to the Welch brothers, Century's list of owners from 1926 to 1961, by contrast, featured a long procession of investors, including Web Sherman, George Eddy, Ard Richardson, Gates Harpel, and Ted Hewitt. Despite the numerous changes in ownership, speed, smart styling, innovative features, and choice African mahogany were consistent hallmarks of Century runabouts and remain as vestiges of Century's wonderful legacy for classic-boat owners today.

began to appear in Century's promotional material. The Sea Maids maintained a similar look but were now identified as 18- and 20-foot models. A new and radical option was a large metal-framed windshield that accommodated a convertible top, hinged on the centerline to provide easier access to the cockpit. Shortly thereafter, however, the Sea Maid name was dropped in favor of the new model designation Arabian for the 18-foot model and Palomino for the 15-foot runabout.

Postwar Century runabouts, such as this 1950 18-foot Resorter, featured an attractive deck pattern of blonde and red mahogan. *Photo by Classic Boating Magazine*

Bibliography

Ballantyne, Philip and Robert Bruce Duncan. *Classic American Runabouts*. Osceola, WI: MBI Publishing Co., 2001.

Brass Bell, The. Chris-Craft Antique Boat Club.

Classic Boating Magazine 1983–2002.

Fostle, D. W. *Speedboat*. Mystic, CT: Mystic Seaport Museum, 1988.

Gribbins, Joseph. *Chris-Craft: A History 1922–1942*. Marblehead, MA: Devereux Books, 2001.

Guétat, Gerald. *Classic Speedboats* 1916–1939. Osceola, WI: MBI Publishing Co., 1997.

Guétat, Gerald. *Classic Speedboats* 1945–1962. Osceola, WI: MBI Publishing Co., 2000.

Pitrone, Jean Maddern and Joan Potter Elwart. *The Dodges*. South Bend, IN: Icarus Press, 1981.

Polmar, Norman and Samuel Morison. *PT Boats at War*. Osceola, WI: MBI Publishing Co., 1999.

Rodengen, Jeffrey L. *The Legend of Chris-Craft*. Ft. Lauderdale, FL: Write Stuff Syndicate, 1993.

Savage, Jack. *Chris-Craft*. Osceola, WI: MBI Publishing Co., 2000.

Speltz, Robert. *The Real Runabouts, Vol. I*. Lake Mills, IA: Graphic Publishing Co., 1977.

Speltz, Robert. *The Real Runabouts, Vol. III*. Lake Mills, IA: Graphic Publishing Co., 1980.

Index

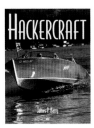
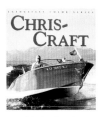
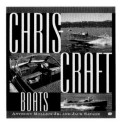
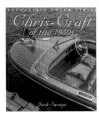

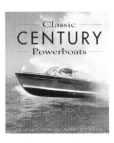
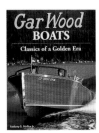
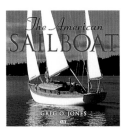
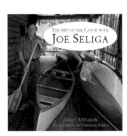